The Waterman/Harewood Piano Series

Piano for Pleasure

Book 1

easy classics – solo and duet

selected and edited by

Fanny Waterman and Marion Harewood

Faber Music Limited

London

Piano for Pleasure follows *Piano Progress* (by the same authors) in providing a graded sequence of pieces by master composers from Bach to Bartók.

Here is an enjoyable, varied repertoire for the pianist who has mastered a basic technique.

Alongside the solo pieces there are duets, which will provide a welcome opportunity for players to enjoy making music with others.

Contents

SOLOS

Georg Philipp Telemann	Dance Galante	3
George Frederick Handel	Minuet in A minor	4
Johann Christoph Bach	Minuet	5
Joseph Haydn	German Dance	6
Daniel Gottlob Türk	The Dancing Master	7
Muzio Clementi	Waltz	8
Wolfgang Amadeus Mozart	Minuet	10
Wolfgang Amadeus Mozart	Allegro	11
Ignaz Pleyel	Minuet and Trio	12
August Eberhard Müller	Serenade	14
Franz Schubert	Ländler	15
Anton Diabelli	Allegretto	16
Michael Ivanovich Glinka	Polka	18
Cornelius Gurlitt	Time for Action	19
Cornelius Gurlitt	In the Meadows	20
Carl Reinecke	Staccato	22
Béla Bartók	Sorrow	23
S. Shevchenko	Spring Day	24
I. Berkovitch	Mazurka	25

(handwritten: Grade II beside Mozart Minuet; Grade III beside August Eberhard Müller Serenade)

DUETS

Ludwig van Beethoven	Ländler	26
Franz Schubert	German Dance	28
Peter Ilyich Tchaikovsky	Waltz	30

This collection © 1989 by Faber Music Ltd
First published in 1989 by Faber Music Ltd
3 Queen Square London WC1N 3AU
Music drawn by Sambo Music Engraving Co
Cover designed by John Bury
Printed in England

Danse Galante

Georg Philipp Telemann
(1681-1767)

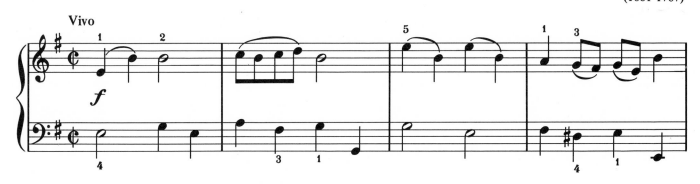

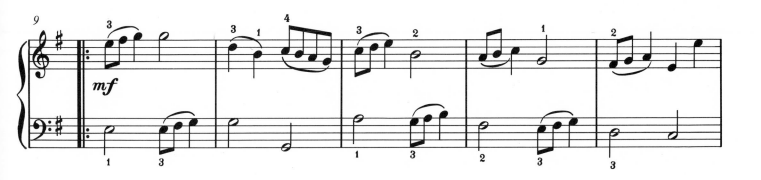

Minuet in A minor

George Frederick Handel
(1685-1759)

Minuet

Johann Christoph Bach
(1732-1795)

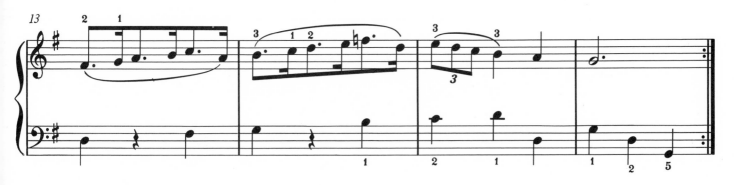

German Dance

Joseph Haydn
(1732-1809)

The Dancing Master

Daniel Gottlob Türk
(1756-1813)

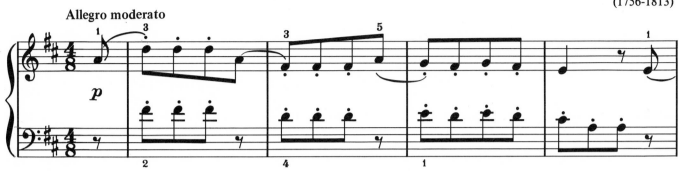

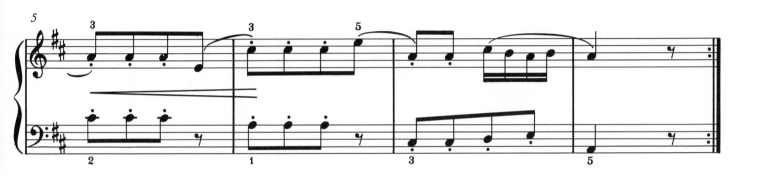

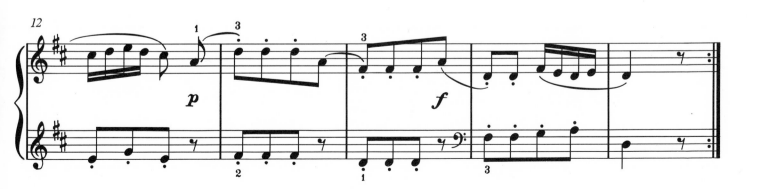

8

Waltz

Muzio Clementi
(1752-1832)

Allegro
K.3

Wolfgang Amadeus Mozart
(1756-1791)

Minuet and Trio

Ignaz Pleyel
(1757-1831)

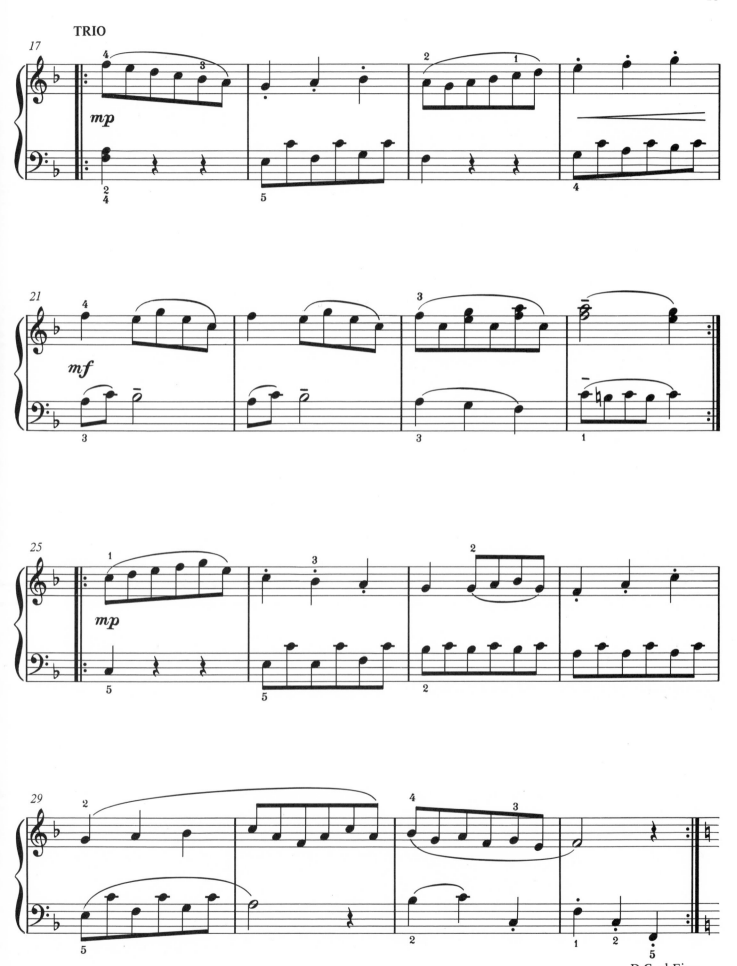

D.C. al Fine

Serenade

August Eberhard Müller
(1767-1817)

Ländler

Franz Schubert
(1797-1828)

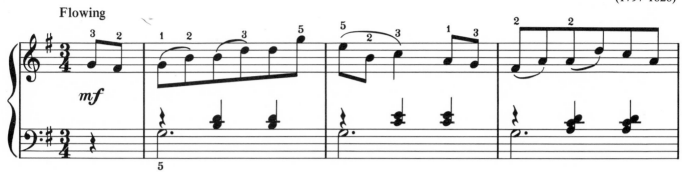

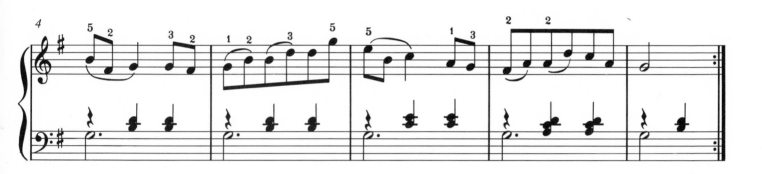

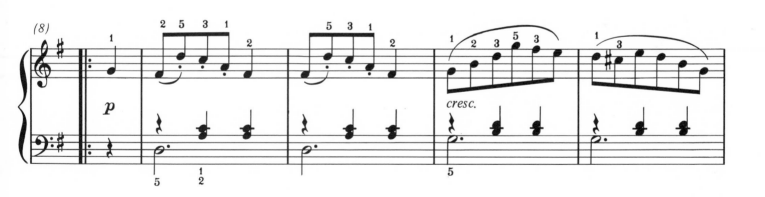

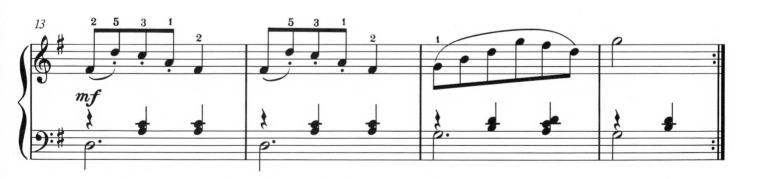

Allegretto
Op.125 No.10

Anton Diabelli
(1781-1858)

Polka

Michael Ivanovich Glinka
(1804-1857)

Time for Action

Cornelius Gurlitt
(1820-1901)

In the Meadows

Cornelius Gurlitt
(1820-1901)

Allegretto scherzando

Staccato

Carl Reinecke
(1824-1910)

Sorrow

Béla Bartók
(1881-1945)

A Spring Day

S. Shevchenko

Mazurka

I. Berkovich

Ländler

SECONDO

Ludwig van Beethoven
(1770-1827)

D.C. al Fine

Ländler

PRIMO

Ludwig van Beethoven
(1770-1827)

D.C. al Fine

German Dance

SECONDO

Franz Schubert
(1797-1828)

German Dance

PRIMO

Franz Schubert
(1797-1828)

Waltz
from Sleeping Beauty

Peter Ilyich Tchaikovsky
(1840-1893)

Waltz
from Sleeping Beauty

Peter Ilyich Tchaikovsky
(1840-1893)

Printed by
Halstan & Co. Ltd., Amersham, Bucks., England